W9-CEW-722

THE ABC's OF Anger

RAY ALI

with
Linda Sander and Jason Kroetsch

Illustrations by Eric Olson

Whole Person Associates
Duluth, Minnesota

Whole Person Associates
210 West Michigan
Duluth, MN 55802
1-800-247-6789

ABC's of Anger

©2006 by Ray Ali. All rights reserved. Except for short excerpts for review purposes, no part of this book may be reproduced or transmitted in any form by any means, electronic or mechanical, including photocopying, without permission in writing from the publisher.

Special Reproduction Policy for Teachers and Group Leaders: Your purchase of this book entitles you to reproduce the illustrations with accompanying text for use in classroom activities. For this use, no additional permission is needed.

Illustrations by Eric Olson

Printed in the United States of America

Library of Congress Control Number: 2005938582

ISBN 1-57025-244-0

ACKNOWLEDGEMENTS

When I first began writing this book, I assumed that it would be a fairly easy and uncomplicated project. It did not take long to realize that this was an extremely foolish assumption. The challenges, however, were eased by the many people who generously gave of their time, expertise, and support. Thanks to all. I'm especially grateful to Jason Kroetsch and Linda Sander, who spent time after work brainstorming with me about the next story and agonizing over which animal and name to use. Your help early in the process is much appreciated.

A huge thanks also to Tia Cummings, who listened to my ramblings and who has an amazing ability to balance praise with constructive criticism. A group of grade three students from Nordale School (Maia, Ryann, Kevin, Charlie, Ben, and Breann) also need to be thanked for reviewing a draft of the book during their lunch breaks. It was a pleasure meeting you and working with you.

Eric Olson and his assistant Katie Cibinel did an incredible job of taking our thoughts and translating them into meaningful and enjoyable illustrations. You gave life to the stories, and for that I am forever grateful.

Finally, I truly appreciate the kindness and professionalism shown to me by the people at Whole Person Associates.

Enjoy!

Ray Ali

INTRODUCTION

"Educating the mind without educating the heart is no education at all."

— Aristotle

In many communities today, lack of respect for self and others seems to be the norm and not the exception. As their exposure to the world widens, children learn values from a variety of sources and experiences. Unfortunately, not all of what they learn from their experiences is desirable. As a result, educators, caregivers, and parents are faced with the monumental task of guiding young people to sift and sort through their beliefs and behaviors, so they can make wise choices.

This book is a resource for early childhood teachers (preschool to grade three), providing them with a wide variety of strategies to use when planning lessons about social and emotional well-being. The book is not meant to be a student workbook, but rather a springboard for teachers to use to initiate discussion and stimulate creative activities that promote student reflection on the topics being covered. This book was written specifically for classroom teachers; however, other childcare specialists as well as parents can readily use it.

ABC's of Anger contains easy-to-read stories involving some aspect of the theme "anger." It provides children with an awareness of differing degrees of anger and helps them explore choices for responding when they are angry.

Each story begins with a letter of the alphabet — the first letter of both an animal's name and its behavior. A picture and short story about the character follow as well as a definition of the characteristic being described. These pictures and stories may be photocopied and distributed for younger children to color and for older students to add cartoon speech balloons. The lesson on the facing page includes questions that the teacher may use to initiate discussion. It is hoped, however, that student responses and questions will lead to a more personalized dialogue with the teacher acting as a discussion facilitator. Follow-up activities conclude each lesson, and these, too, may be adapted to suit the needs of the class.

A resource chapter at the end of the book further explains the theme words and provides additional questions for classroom use.

The stories may be read separately or can be combined into themes, such as trigger words, anger intensity words, solution words, empowering words, and feeling words.

The characters in the stories are designed to help students make connections between their own actions and feelings as well as those that they may experience in other children and adults. We hope that this book will challenge children's thinking and provide a nonthreatening means for them to work through feelings, behaviors, and emotions in a beneficial and enjoyable way.

Anton Alligator used to be a lot of fun to be around. He isn't fun to be around anymore. Now he comes to school grumpy and doesn't want to play with his old friends. In fact, he doesn't play with anyone. He looks and acts angry and even walks as if he is mad at everyone. Just the other day someone accidentally bumped into him, and he got so mad he began to yell and swear. He also shows his anger by not listening in class and by playing really rough on the playground. His friends want to help him get "un-angry."

Discussion Starters

1 Close your eyes and remember a time when someone was angry at you. What did you do?

2 What does being really, really angry look like? What does it feel like? What does it sound like?

3 Is it okay to feel anger? Is it okay to act angry?

4 How can anger sometimes hurt friendships?

5 Can you think of a time when you were proud of the way you expressed your anger?

6 What could you do to help Anton deal with his anger?

Anger

is a feeling that needs to be expressed in ways that do not cause problems for you.

Things To Do

 Ask students to draw three faces: the first showing a little anger, the second showing medium anger, and the third showing big anger. Discuss the differences in the faces.

Conclude a discussion about anger by asking the class to make a poster of words and phrases people use instead of saying the word anger. See if they can find words beginning with each letter of the alphabet, such as A = aggression, B = bully and so on.

Bertha Bear has some nice qualities about her, but she also has a bad reputation for bullying other children. No wonder Bertha does not have many friends in her school. In fact, the only kids she hangs around with are those who think it is "real cool" to bully others. Bertha is very careful about who she bullies. During recess, she is never mean to big, strong kids. Instead, she likes to bully one classmate who is shy and much smaller than she is. Bertha thinks it is funny, but it is not. It has to stop!

Discussion Starters

1 Close your eyes and recall the last time you saw someone being a bully.

2 What can you do to prevent yourself from being bullied?

3 What is the difference between "bully behavior" and "having fun" or "teasing"?

4 What needs are being met by someone who bullies? How can they meet those needs in a different way?

5 What can you do to keep someone from being bullied?

6 What can you do to help someone like Bertha stop bullying others?

B

Bullying

is using your power to persistently and intentionally hurt someone weaker than you are.

Things To Do

 Suggest that students watch their favorite TV shows and look for people who act like bullies.

 Discuss with the students ways to "bully proof" your classroom.

Carlos Camel was so excited to show his parents a letter from his teacher that he ran home without stopping. He was very proud, and he knew that his parents would be proud of him as well. The letter said:

Dear Carlos:

I am writing this letter to let you know how very pleased I am with your attitude and behavior this month. Your listening skills are terrific! During this time, I have not had any reason to ask you to leave class for misbehaving. It seems to me that you are more confident, more relaxed, and friendlier to be around. The reason is clear to me: you have found ways to chill out before you get angry. Congratulations Chill-out Champion!

From your Teacher

Discussion Starters

To **chill out** is to calm down and prevent an angry outburst.

1 Close your eyes and recall a time that you were angry but did something to calm yourself down.

2 What chill-out strategies work best for you?

3 Can you think of a chill-out strategy that you would like to practice?

4 Why is listening a good chill-out strategy?

5 What are some of the good things that can happen to Carlos now that he is able to tame his anger?

6 Carlos's teacher had noticed his change in behavior. Who else do you think noticed?

Things To Do

 Ask students to draw a tree, naming each branch with a chill-out idea, such as plan ahead, relax, think, and listen. Suggest that they post the picture tree on their bedroom wall.

Make a master list of all the chill-out ideas that your class can come up with. Display it on the wall. Add to the list when a new idea emerges.

Dana Dingo is known as a daredevil. She'll try anything, especially on a dare. She does this to impress her friends. There are times, however, when her daredevil stunts become foolish and scary to watch. She becomes especially reckless when she is angry. Once she took her skateboard and left the school grounds without permission so she could show how tough she was. If she doesn't stop, she is going to get into real big trouble or even hurt herself or someone else.

Discussion Starters

1 Think of someone who is a daredevil. Describe this person without using his or her name.

2 What is the difference between taking a risk and being a daredevil?

3 When is being a daredevil a good idea? When is it not a good idea?

4 What might happen if you are angry and someone asks you to do a daredevil activity?

5 What needs are being met by being a daredevil?

6 Why is leaving the school grounds without permission a wrong choice for Dana?

A

daredevil

is someone who likes doing dangerous, risky, and often unsafe activities.

Things To Do

 Read a storybook about a famous daredevil.
Ask students to listen for what the daredevil's safety plan is.

 Discuss with your class concepts like risk-taking, pranks, adventures, challenges, and dares.

Edgar Elephant is a caring and compassionate boy who has many friends. It is easy to understand why. When you have a problem, you can always count on Edgar to listen to you. He may not have all the answers, but you feel much better after talking to him. Edgar knows that caring through listening is an important way to show empathy. Other ways he shows empathy are by volunteering his time in lots of school activities and helping those less fortunate than he is.

Discussion Starters

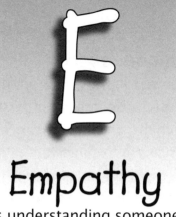

E

Empathy

is understanding someone else's feelings, moods, and experiences.

1 Close your eyes and think of the person who understands you the best. Would you like to be like that person? Why?

2 Describe a situation when you showed empathy to someone.

3 How could you show empathy towards an animal?

4 Why is showing empathy towards others a good thing to do?

5 When you are feeling sad or angry or worried or disappointed, how would you like others to treat you?

6 What kind of body language was Edgar using to show that he was listening with empathy?

Things to Do

 Suggest that students create emotion puppets, make up a story, and put on a play. Simple puppets can be made by drawing faces to show feelings, such as sadness, happiness, and anger. Cut out the faces and glue them on Popsicle sticks.

 Play emotional charades. Develop a list of words to describe emotions. Have students randomly choose one of the emotions to act out without using words. See if the class can guess the word.

Fernando Fox was looking forward to the school's winter carnival. Unfortunately, the weather turned frightfully cold, and the winter carnival had to be cancelled. Everyone was terribly disappointed, especially Fernando. When Fernando was told about the cancellation, he became furious. He threw all of his books on the floor and yelled at the teacher that she was "stupid and mean." His teacher did not like being called these names, but she understood his disappointment and was able to help Fernando calm down and talk about his feelings. After a few minutes, Fernando returned to his class and even helped plan an indoor winter carnival for the afternoon.

Being
furious
is having strong, angry feelings.

Discussion Starters

1 Describe a time when you were furious.
What made you feel that way?

2 Last time you were furious, could you have
acted differently?

3 Are there good reasons to be furious?
Are there bad reasons to be furious?

4 What does furious look like? What does it feel like?
What does it sound like?

5 How can being furious be hurtful to yourself
or others?

6 What do you think the teacher said to Fernando
to help him calm down?

Things to Do

Ask students to draw a picture of someone who is furious.
Is being furious the same thing as being angry?

Draw an "Anger Thermometer" and give it to your class.
At the bottom print the number "1" and the words "little angry."
At the top print the number "10" and the words "very, very angry."
What words would you use to describe numbers 2 to 9?
What number would you give the word "furious"?

Glenda Giraffe is very generous with her time and is a good sharer. Everyone in her class can tell a personal story about her helpfulness. For example, one day she shared her sandwich and banana with a classmate who forgot his lunch. Another time she helped her friend complete her science fair project. "It feels good to help others" is the way she explains her unselfishness. Everyone likes her because of her giving nature. Glenda finds that when she is generous with others, they are, in turn, generous with her.

Discussion Starters

To be
generous
is to give more
than is expected.

1 Close your eyes and think of a generous person. What does that person do that makes them generous?

2 Describe a time when you were generous to others.

3 How can being generous help someone who is angry?

4 What needs are being met when you are generous?

5 When is it hard to be generous?

6 If you are as generous as Glenda, what does that say about you?

Things to Do

 Suggest that students be generous to each member of their family without telling them. A couple days later, ask whether their parents, brothers, and sisters noticed their generosity.

 Create a project that allows your class to be generous to others in need.

19

When **Herschel Hyena** is told to do something that he does not like, or if he doesn't get what he wants, he throws a hissy fit. He squints; his face reddens; and he stomps his feet really fast. His hissy fits don't help him, and they are very annoying for others to watch. For example, one afternoon after art class, his teacher asked him to clean up his art station. Everyone knows that you have to clean up before you go out for recess. Instead of putting things away, he threw a hissy fit that lasted the whole recess. Not only did he not go out for recess, he still had to put away his art materials.

Discussion Starters

1. Close your eyes and imagine someone who is having a hissy fit. What is this person saying and doing?

2. Share a story about when you threw a hissy fit, and it did not work.

3. How do you feel when you are having a hissy fit?

4. How do you feel when you see someone else throwing a hissy fit?

5. How can throwing a hissy fit be harmful to you or harmful to others?

6. Why do you think Herschel throws hissy fits? What do you think he can do to stop himself from doing this?

A
hissy fit
is similar to
a temper tantrum.

Things to Do

 Suggest that students practice throwing a hissy fit while looking at themselves in a mirror. What do they see?

 Role-play a situation in which someone is throwing a hissy fit. Brainstorm ways to help this person.

Today was going to be the biggest soccer match of the year. During recess time, the two best teams were going to compete to see which would be the school champion. The problem was deciding who would referee the game — more importantly, who could referee and be fair. The answer was obvious. The team captains asked **Imarika Iguana**. Not only did she understand the rules of the game, but also, she was seen as being impartial. She agreed to referee with one condition: there would be no arguments after the game. Even though it would be a challenge, she felt that she could do the job fairly and not favor one team over the other. This was going to test her ability, because she had friends on both sides. After the game, both teams congratulated her for being impartial.

Discussion Starters

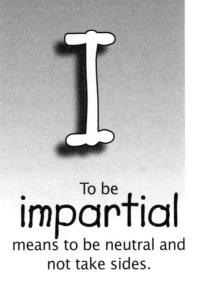

To be
impartial
means to be neutral and
not take sides.

1 Close your eyes and recall a time when you or someone else was impartial.

2 Describe a situation when you or someone else was not being impartial.

3 When do you find it difficult to be impartial?

4 What are some good consequences of being impartial?

5 How can acting impartial help others from getting angry?

6 What could have happened at the game if Imarika was not impartial?

Things to Do

 Remind students who play sports that require a referee to thank the referee at the end of the game for a job well done and for being impartial.

 Brainstorm with your class a list of jobs in which being impartial is important.

Jenny Jellyfish does not like coming to school anymore. It all started when a new girl by the name of Jasmine joined the class. Within a short period of time, Jasmine became very popular. She was smart, fun to be with, and excellent in sports. Jenny became increasingly jealous of Jasmine's popularity and was afraid that she could not compete with her. She felt that she would lose all of her friends. Her jealousy became so strong that she wanted to do something really mean to Jasmine. Jenny knew that these feelings were creating problems, and she had to tell someone about them before she got into really big trouble.

Discussion Starters

Jealousy

is the upset feeling you have because you want something that someone else has.

1 Close your eyes and remember a time when you felt very jealous.

2 How did your jealousy go away?

3 How are anger and jealousy the same? How are they different?

4 How can being jealous be hurtful to you or hurtful to others?

5 Do you think that people are jealous of you? Why do you think that way?

6 Finish the story with Jenny solving her problem of jealousy.

Things to Do

 Teach students how to write an acrostic poem using the word jealousy.

 Discuss with your class the words jealousy and envy. Compare these words with other words like admiration and respect.

Katrina Koala's class has an important rule: "Always be kind to others with your words and actions." Even on days when she is unhappy or upset, she reminds herself that it is better to be kind to others than to be disrespectful. For Katrina, this is the best way to live at home as well as at school. She feels good inside knowing that she has helped someone. Katrina ended a classroom speech by saying, "Kind is hard to describe, but everyone knows it when they see it."

Discussion Starters

Being kind is being friendly, caring, and helpful to other people.

1 Close your eyes and think of the kindest person you know.

2 Can you describe a time when you were kind to someone else? How did you feel?

3 How do you feel when someone is kind to you?

4 How can being kind be helpful to someone who is angry?

5 How can you be kind to yourself?

6 What do you think Katrina's class is doing to be kind to others?

Things to Do

 Ask the entire class to pay special attention to good manners. They should say "hello" to everyone and remember to say "excuse me," "please," and "thank you." At the end of the school day, discuss whether the day went better when everyone was kind and thoughtful.

 Plan a "random act of kindness day." Ask students to do something kind for another child. At the end of the day, have a discussion on kindness. Make a list of all the kind deeds done. Pay attention to feelings associated with kindness.

Lincoln Lion is good at listening. Lincoln had learned that to be a good listener you have to be patient and attentive. When someone talks, he listens to everything they have to say before he responds. He also knows that it is important to pay attention to their body language. This helps him to understand the concerns of his friends and not jump to conclusions. Being a good listener helps Lincoln be a great problem solver. He also knows that being a good listener helps people to calm down when they are angry.

Discussion Starters

1 What do you do with your body when you are actively listening?

2 How can you tell by watching body language that someone is angry?

3 How can listening reduce anger?

4 Describe a time when listening was hard to do.

5 How would you describe your listening skills? Are there things you can do to improve your listening skills?

6 What do you think Lincoln does to be a good listener?

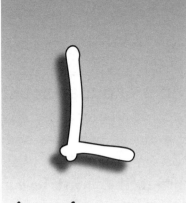

Listening
is concentrating and paying attention when someone is talking to you.

Things to Do

 This memory game teaches students to listen carefully. Form a circle and ask the first student to begin by saying, "I'm going to the store and I'm going to buy (name an item)." The person to the right of the speaker continues by saying, "I'm going to the store and I'm going to buy (the first person's item and a new item)." Continue around the circle to see how many items each person can remember.

 To practice the art of listening, divide the class into pairs. Ask student A to tell a story to student B without interruptions. When the story is finished, student B should retell it as accurately as possible. They should then reverse roles.

Misa Mouse has discovered a good way to relax. She uses meditation. Each day before she goes to bed, she spends a few minutes by herself. She closes her eyes and thinks about the good things that happened to her during the day. Misa practices deep breathing and allows her mind to think of her most favourite place. She believes that this helps her to calm down, to unwind, and to concentrate. When Misa finds herself getting really angry, she practices her meditation exercises. They work.

Discussion Starters

Meditation is a way to relax and feel calm.

1. Have you ever seen someone meditate? How do you think that would feel?

2. Think of a time when deep breathing or closing your eyes would have been helpful to you.

3. What activities do you do to relax? Have you ever tried relaxing or calming yourself before an activity or before taking a school test?

4. How can meditating be helpful to you?

5. If you closed your eyes and thought about your favorite place, what would that place look like, feel like, and sound like?

6. How does meditation help Misa calm down, especially when she is getting angry?

Things to Do

 Lead students in this easy breathing exercise:

> Sit in a comfortable position.
> Breathe deeply into your tummy.
> Wait for two seconds before breathing out.
> As you breathe out, count "one" to yourself.
> Slowly breathe in and out again, counting "two."
> Continue breathing and counting until you reach ten.

 Begin each morning by leading your class in a relaxation exercise. Make it part of your daily routine.

Nelson Narwhal has been learning all about nutrition in health class at school. He learned that he needs to eat balanced meals with nutritious snacks in between. Instead of eating chocolate bars or drinking soft drinks, he now chooses to eat such things as fruit and yogurt. Nelson discovered that when he eats too much junk food, he gets cranky and tired. He learned that his body needs "food fuel" throughout the day if he is going to be active and attentive. All of the healthy food that Nelson eats each day is helping to make his mind and body stronger.

Discussion Starters

1 Close your eyes and see in front of you a tasty and nutritious breakfast, lunch, and supper.

2 How would you describe your eating habits?

3 If you ate only junk food, what would happen to your body? What would happen to your mind? What would happen to your feelings?

4 What is the difference between a nutritious snack and one that is not?

5 List five nutritious snacks.

6 Why do you think eating well, as Nelson did, makes your mind and body strong?

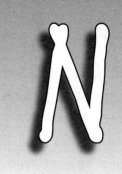

Good
nutrition
means eating foods and drinks that are good for you.

Things to Do

 Ask students to keep a food journal. On a specific day, have them list in their journals everything that they eat and drink. The next day, they should look over the list and circle the foods that are nutritious.

 Have your class create a menu for a restaurant that serves only nutritious foods.

Olivia Octopus is teaching her friend Frank to be organized. Frank is not very organized, which explains why he loses things and is often late for his activities. When this happens, he always gets frustrated or angry. The first thing Olivia did was help Frank organize his school desk and backpack. Olivia explained to him that items like rulers and pencils should each have a special place. When you put them in their place, they are easy to find when you need them. Olivia says that when she is organized, learning is much easier.

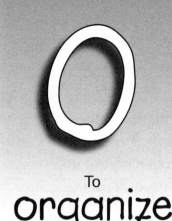

To
organize
is to put things away in their proper place.

Discussion Starters

1 Close your eyes and imagine that your desk is super organized. Is this picture different than the way your desk really is right now?

2 What are some things you do now to be organized?

3 What are some other things you could do to make yourself more organized?

4 Why do some people get angry when they are not organized?

5 How can being more organized be helpful to you or others?

6 Why does Olivia believe being organized makes learning easier?

Things to Do

 Ask students to spend time this week organizing their dresser drawers. Suggest that they invite a member of their family to help.

 Have your students create a homework checklist and tape it on their desk or locker. Make sure they check this list every day before they leave school.

Perla Porcupine realized that she was not good at problem solving. She was often in too much of a hurry to find an effective solution. Occasionally her solutions created more problems than they solved. One day, she and her friends were at a bonfire and wanted to roast marshmallows, but they did not have any sticks. This time, instead of getting angry, Perla realized that she should stop and think carefully. She did, and she came up with a great solution.

Discussion Starters

1. Close your eyes and think of someone who you know is a good problem solver. What makes him or her a good problem solver?

2. Describe a time when you solved a problem. What steps did you take?

3. How can problem solving help you make better choices when you are angry?

4. How can you help others to problem solve?

5. What does it say about Perla now that she is practicing problem solving?

6. What was Perla's solution?

Problem solving

is a way of finding effective solutions.

Things to Do

 Before sending students out for recess, ask them to see if they can help someone on the playground problem solve.

 Teach students the steps of problem solving, which are listed on pages 59 and 60. Make a poster listing these steps and display it on a wall. Give students opportunities to practice or role-play the steps, and then create situations containing problems for them to solve.

Quinton Quail loves to play checkers, but cannot find anyone to play with. All of the other students have told Quinton that they will not play with him because he gets mad and quits when he is losing. He now has a reputation for being a sore loser. Quinton has been thinking about what the other children told him, and he knows that it's true. Quinton wants to fix his problem so that he can play checkers and have fun. He no longer wants to be known as a sore loser.

Discussion Starters

1 Close your eyes and recall a time when you quit a game because you were angry.

2 Why do you think some people quit games when they are losing?

3 Have you ever played a game when someone quit?
Why do you think this happened?
How did it make you feel?

4 Is there a good time to quit an activity?
Is there a bad time to quit an activity?

5 How do you think Quinton feels when he is losing?

6 What could you do to help Quinton have fun when he is playing checkers?

To
quit

is to stop doing something.

Things to Do

Ask students to draw a comic strip showing a time when they got upset and quit an activity in a bad way. Then have them redraw the final panel to show a better way to handle their anger.

Discuss with your class good ways to quit and bad ways to quit. Introduce concepts of a gracious winner and a sore loser. Also inquire if there are such things as bad winners and good losers.

When **Rachael Rabbit** gets steaming mad at a friend, she has a terrible habit of starting rumors about that person. Rachael thinks that it's okay to spread rumors because she is just getting back at her friend. Sometimes she makes up a story about someone and passes it on to her friends. Sometimes she spreads rumors using her computer. Her friends know that she does this, and now they don't trust her with secrets. If Rachael Rabbit does not stop spreading rumors, she will lose her friends.

Discussion Starters

Rumors

are stories, often untrue, that are spread from one person to another.

1 Close your eyes and imagine that someone was spreading rumors about you. How does this make you feel?

2 Is spreading rumors the same thing as telling lies?

3 How can spreading rumors be hurtful to you? How can it be hurtful to others?

4 Why do some kids spread rumors when they are angry?

5 What would you do if your friend told you a rumor that you knew was not true?

6 How could you help Rachael stop spreading rumors?

Things to Do

 The best way to stop rumors is to not begin them and not pass them on. Challenge students to go an entire day without spreading rumors.

 Demonstrate how rumors can change the truth by having your class participate in the rumor game. Whisper a story to one student. Have that student repeat the story to another student, changing it slightly to make it more exciting. Have student two tell the story to student three, again changing it a bit. Continue until student six has heard the story; then have student six share the story with the group. Compare the final story with the original.

Sammy Shark often talks back to the teacher in a rude and sassy way. Sometimes he says things when he is frustrated and angry; while other times he says things to be funny or to get attention. One way he shows his sassiness is by mimicking his teacher, but his friends don't always laugh, especially when the things that Sammy says are disrespectful and hurtful. His sassiness often gets him into trouble, and at times, he has to leave the classroom.

Discussion Starters

Being
sassy
is talking back
in a rude way.

1 Close your eyes and remember a time
when you were sassy to someone.

2 What does sassy look like? What does it feel like?
What does it sound like?

3 How do you feel when someone like Sammy
is sassy to you?

4 How can you stop yourself from being sassy?

5 Can adults be sassy too?

6 What can Sammy do to stop himself
from being sassy?

Things to Do

 Have students create a recipe for Sassy Soup, asking
them to select ingredients and then speculate on
how the soup will taste.

 On the chalkboard, draw the outlines of two people.
With your students, generate a list of synonyms for sassy,
such as rudeness and back-talk and write them on or around
one of the figures. On the second figure, list their opposites.
Discuss with your students which person they would rather be.

Thunder Turtle realized that when he got really angry he would get into big trouble. One afternoon his teacher sat down with him and discussed some options for Thunder to consider. He thought about what his teacher said, and together they developed a time-out plan. Now, before he gets really angry, he gives himself a time-out. When he is angry in his classroom, he tells his teacher that he needs a time-out to cool off. He goes into the hallway, and when he feels calm, he re-enters the class. What a good solution for Thunder and his teacher!

Discussion Starters

1 Describe a situation when you took or should have taken a time-out.

2 Describe a situation when an adult took or should have taken a time-out.

3 Why is taking a time-out a good thing to do?

4 How does taking a time-out help reduce anger?

5 What are the steps for taking a time-out?

6 What can Thunder think about when he is taking a time-out?

A

time-out

is a way to slow down and think things over.

Things to Do

 Invite students to draw pictures of creative time-outs for their sisters, brothers, parents, and themselves.

 Discuss with students the purpose of a time-out. Develop together a list of steps to take when students need a time-out and while they are taking one. Display the list in your classroom.

Uma Unicorn is uncooperative in gym class. She does not listen to instructions and gets frustrated when she cannot do an activity as well as her classmates. She is especially unreasonable when she has to do an activity that she does not like. She does not pay attention; she acts silly; and at times is so disruptive that she is asked to leave the gym. When she is like this, it is difficult to be her friend or even to be nice to her because she is not pleasant to be around. She would probably have more fun if she cooperated.

Discussion Starters

1 Close your eyes and describe a time when someone was uncooperative at school.

2 Share a story about when you were uncooperative.

3 How can being uncooperative lead to anger?

4 What does being uncooperative feel like? What does it sound like? What does it look like?

5 Why do you think Uma is uncooperative during gym class?

6 What can Uma do to be more cooperative?

Being
uncooperative
is not doing things
that you should be doing.

Things to Do

 Encourage students to help their friends be more cooperative by using a role-play activity. Form small groups, and then give one person in each group a slip of paper with an "I won't" statement, such as "I won't sing in the holiday program" or "I won't go skating." The other members of the group should try to persuade this student to cooperate. Share the most effective ideas with the entire class.

Provide magazines and ask students to create individual or group collages that show people cooperating.

Vinit Vulture, Wanda Weasel, and **Xu Xenops** are the best of friends. When they are angry they each choose a favorite activity to relax and blow off steam. Vinit plays volleyball; Wanda writes in her journal; and Xu plays the xylophone. When they finish their activities, they often find that their anger has disappeared. Aren't they smart to have found time-out activities that work for them?

Discussion Starters

1 Why is engaging in an activity helpful in lowering your anger?

2 What activities do you do, or can you do, to blow off steam?

3 Are there times when doing an activity may make your anger grow even bigger?

4 What should you do when you are angry before playing a game?

5 What activity does your best friend use to chill out?

6 Why do you think activities help Vinit, Wanda and Xu to get rid of their anger?

Things to Do

 Ask students to think of a favorite activity that their classmates might not know about. As they take turns acting out their activity, those watching should try to guess what it is. When it has been guessed, have them explain why they enjoy it.

 Invite your class to bring in photos of themselves engaged in various activities. Display them all on a poster.

Everyone knows when **Yves Yak** is angry and upset. His voice gets louder and louder. Then, when he is really mad, he begins to yell at the top of his voice. His eyes get bigger; his face gets redder; and his body tenses. His yelling scares people because he says mean things. When he yells, he cannot listen to what others are saying. Yelling is anger talking. Yves needs to find ways to stop yelling.

Discussion Starters

Y
Yelling
is talking loudly,
angrily, and rudely.

1 Close your eyes and think of a time when people
were yelling at one another. What would you
like to say to them to make them stop?

2 When is yelling okay?

3 What does it feel like when someone
is yelling at you?

4 Think of a time when you were angry and yelling
at someone. How did you feel after you
calmed down?

5 Why is yelling not a good way of getting
your point across?

6 How can you stop yourself from yelling?
How could you help Yves from yelling?

Things to Do

Read short passages from a children's book using different
voice levels, from whispering to yelling. Ask students
which voice level they like best and why.

Divide the class into three groups. Have one group solve
a problem by talking very quietly; ask another group to
use a normal voice; while the third group should only yell.
After a few minutes, discuss which voice was
the most effective.

Zobida Zebra is always fun to be with because of her zany behaviors. You simply do not know what she will do next! Some days she wears silly clothes or tells funny stories. Whatever she does, it brightens up the day. Even though she does zany things, she would never hurt anyone's feelings, embarrass them, or get them into trouble. She knows the difference between doing zany things and doing dangerous activities.

Discussion Starters

1 Close your eyes and think of a cartoon character that you would describe as zany. What does he or she do that makes him or her zany?

2 Share a story about a zany thing that you did recently.

3 What is the difference between being zany and being annoying?

4 What are the reactions of your friends when you are acting zany?

5 Can you think of a zany thing that you can do today?

6 Do you have a friend like Zobida who does zany things? How do you feel when you are with her?

Being

zany

is being funny in an unusual and crazy way.

Things to Do

 With your students, brainstorm a list of zany activities that would make their families laugh. Have students review the list and delete any items that might be dangerous, hurt anyone's feelings, or get them in trouble. Encourage them to select one of the remaining activities and try it at home, reporting the next day on whether their families thought it was funny.

 Plan a zany-day activity with your class. For example, plan a weird-dress day.

Discussion Questions, Tips, and Activities

The information and questions that follow provide additional resources for teaching children about anger and how to manage it. We encourage you to use many creative ways to engage students, such as role playing, drawing, making collages, story telling, and writing. The primary goal is to stimulate conversation and to help children develop greater awareness of their feelings, thoughts, and actions.

ANGER

As educators, it is crucial that we continually help children understand and express their emotions. Anger is one of those emotions. We need to differentiate between angry feelings and the choices we make as a result of being angry. Anger, as a feeling, is a human response that tells us something is wrong and needs to be changed. From this perspective, anger may be positive in that it creates passion. Feelings of anger do not get us into trouble. What gets us into trouble are the bad choices we make as a result of our anger. A good phrase to use is "mad not bad." We have the right to be mad, but we do not have the right to be bad.

Anger becomes a problem when it has the following characteristics: It is too intense for the situation; it lasts too long; it happens too frequently; it hurts relationships; and it impairs school performance.

Additional questions for discussion:

- How do you feel when a friend changes his or her friendship group? Does it make you angry, sad, or confused?
- How do you know when someone is angry with you?
- Does it feel different when a friend, rather than a brother, sister, or parent, is angry with you?
- What can you do if you come to school angry because of something that happened at home?
- What can you do if you go home angry because of something that happened at school?

BULLY

Bullying is an increasing concern in many schools, and sadly this issue presents itself at every grade level. We are beginning to understand the signs of bullying and are becoming more aware of its impact on those affected by it — both the bullies and their victims. It is important that this issue be discussed in every classroom.

Bullying may involve physical violence, threats, extortion, teasing, humiliation, shunning, or hurtful rumors. To reduce it, try some of the following ideas:

- Identify specific situations that describe bully behaviors.
- Be familiar with the signs of bullying.
- Send a strong message that bullying is not tolerated.
- Develop strategies for bullies, for their victims, and for those who observe bullying.
- Monitor unstructured times such as recess and lunch hour as well as hallway activities.
- Involve parents in developing programs and policies to create classrooms and schools that are "bully-free zones."

Additional questions for discussion:

- What does it feel like to be bullied?
- Why do kids bully others? What do they have to gain?
- Why are some kids bullied more often than others?
- Is there a difference between how boys and girls bully?
- Why do bullies think it is okay or funny to bully others?
- How does a bully choose someone to bully?

CHILL-OUT

It's important to help children develop a wide range of options to implement when their anger is becoming a problem. Chill-outs are ways to slow things down, to cool off, and to give time to assess the situation in order to make better choices. Children need to learn ways to monitor their anger. We can help by encouraging them to talk about their triggers, the way they process or interpret information, their negative self-talk, their underlying feelings, and the choices they make.

Additional questions for discussion:

- What can you do when you first notice that you are getting angry?
- What can you do when you are already angry?
- What can you do after you calm down?

DAREDEVIL

Children are always testing their personal boundaries, and it is important that we encourage these explorations. We want children to experiment and to take risks, but not to the point of jeopardizing their safety or the safety of others. We want them to be able to distinguish risks that are healthy from those that are not. Healthy risks involve planning, organization, practice, perseverance, and a strong desire to succeed. Poor risks are generally based on showing off, being impulsive, or doing something that is beyond one's capability. Children need to avoid taking risks when they are angry and not thinking clearly. They need to find ways to say no when confronted with a dare that places them at risk. They also need ways to dissuade their friends when they are doing a foolish daredevil activity.

Additional questions for discussion:

- How can you be a wise daredevil?
- What can you do to make a daredevil activity safe?
- How can you say "no" to a dare that is unsafe?
- Why are dares particularly unsafe when you are angry?
- What kinds of trouble can you get into as a result of daredevil activities?
- What can you do to stop a friend from doing a foolish daredevil stunt?

EMPATHY

Empathy is the capacity to understand someone else's feelings, words, and actions. It is an important social skill, and research has shown that children who are empathic tend to be trusted, better liked, and have more friends. It is truly the ability to "walk a mile in another person's shoes." Children who are frequently angry tend to have a diminished capacity to be empathic. Listening is the cornerstone to empathy. Listening is more than understanding words. It is also about paying attention to feelings and body language.

Encourage your students to volunteer in age-appropriate volunteer activities and involve the class in charitable causes.

Additional questions for discussion:

- How does one become empathic?
- Why is it easier to talk to someone who you really trust and respect?
- How does empathy promote closer friendships?
- How do you show your friends that you truly understand them?
- What does "walk a mile in another person's shoes" mean?
- Why is volunteering important?

FURIOUS

Being furious is often connected with being disappointed in someone or something. Typically it takes the form of blaming, being argumentative, and at times being unmanageable. At these times children need time to vent and rant before you can talk to them. It takes patience to quietly listen to them. If they become too disruptive, however, it is best to isolate them from others. The key is to teach them how to manage their emotions when they become disappointed.

Additional questions for discussion:

- How would you describe Fernando's feelings when he learned that the winter carnival was cancelled?
- Describe a time when you were disappointed. What did you do?
- Why do we often say mean things when we are angry?
- What can we do or say to apologize to someone we were mean to?
- What is the best way for you to calm down when you are furious?
- What do you do to help friends who are furious when they don't get their way?

GENEROUS

Generosity is about sharing. It is about observing the needs of others and where possible filling those needs by being generous with time, ideas and material things. Generosity is about providing these things without asking for anything in return. Being generous is one of the anchors of being a good friend and being a good citizen. Children need to be generous to others, and they also need to be able to communicate their appreciation when someone is generous to them.

Additional questions for discussion:

- Why is generosity an important quality of friendship?
- Why is it important to thank someone for helping you?
- Do you find it difficult to be generous to some people?
- Is it difficult to be generous with someone you do not like?
- What emotions do you experience when you are generous with others?
- Is there such a thing as being too generous?

HISSY FIT

Hissy fits are temper tantrums used by children to manipulate adults and get their own way. They are annoying to watch and can test one's patience. The important point is not to give in to the demands of the child. Fortunately a hissy fit doesn't last long, and it's best to respond to a child only when the tantrum is over. However, it is important that during moments of rage, the child's safety and the safety of others are ensured.

Additional questions for discussion:
- How would you describe a hissy fit?
- Is there such a thing as being too old to throw a hissy fit?
- What can you do to stop a friend from having a hissy fit?
- How is a hissy fit the same or different from being angry?
- How can being angry turn into a hissy fit?

IMPARTIAL

To be impartial is to be fair and honest. It is a skill that requires an understanding of the rules of a game and the strength of character to not take sides. Children often get angry when they think they are being cheated, and at times they need someone they can trust to mediate a dispute — someone who is impartial.

Additional questions for discussion:
- Why is it important to be fair?
- Why is it wrong to be unfair?
- Why is it important to know the rules of a game if you are going to be impartial?
- How can being unfair lead to someone getting angry?
- When is it difficult to be impartial?

JEALOUSY

Jealousy is a serious problem for some children and left unchecked can lead to emotional and relationship difficulties. There is a strong correlation between jealousy and low self-esteem, aggression, anger, and loneliness. You can help children avoid jealousy by encouraging them to be confident and independent, strengthening their social skills, practicing empathy with them, and teaching them to avoid critical and harmful negative self-talk.

It is important to teach children the following:
- Everyone is different.
- Sometimes we can not get what we want.
- Be yourself.
- Jealousy tends to be hurtful to the person who is jealous.
- Sometimes jealousy is disguised as anger.
- Stop making inaccurate comparisons.

Additional questions for discussion:
- Why are some kids more jealous than others are?
- Where does jealousy come from?
- What can you do to stop yourself from becoming jealous?

- How can jealousy hurt friendships?
- How can being jealous start hurtful rumors?

KIND

A single act can be described as kind, or the word can describe a person's overall character. If you perform many kind acts, you will be identified as a kind person. Children often show acts of kindness and should be complimented for these acts. Other words related to kindness are respect, caring, responsibility, and generosity.

Additional questions for discussion:
- What are some of the things you do that can be considered kind?
- What is the similarity between being kind and being generous?
- How can being kind make you feel good inside?
- What does it mean when you describe somebody as a kind person?
- Why is being kind important to friendships?

LISTENING

Active listening is an art and is fundamental to good communication. To listen is not only to hear the words that are being spoken but also to understand the person's feelings through the words. A good listener is attentive and responsive and focuses on the other person throughout the conversation.

Good listeners:
- Show interest and are attentive to the person speaking.
- Avoid distractions and interruptions.
- Nod or give verbal cues to encourage the speaker to continue talking.
- Clarify and restate what they have heard.
- Pay attention to nonverbal clues.

Additional questions for discussion:
- What are nonverbal messages?
- Why is being patient important if you are to be a good listener?
- Why is it important not to interrupt before someone finishes speaking?
- Why does good listening help problem solving?
- How can listening to people help them to calm down?

MEDITATION

Meditation provides an opportunity to reflect, take time to review the day, and to be alone with your thoughts. Meditation encourages us to connect with our inner self by making quiet time for ourselves. It is an opportunity to be in a space for problem solving and determining the direction in which we should move. It is also a good way to defuse anger and calm down.

Meditaion can be induced by deep breathing, mental imagery, relaxation exercises, and positive affirmation. It would be beneficial to students to start or end the school day with a relaxing deep-breathing exercise.

Additional questions for discussion:
- Why do you think that it is a good idea to spend a few minutes to review your day and to think about tomorrow?
- Is meditation a silly thing to do?
- Do you think your friends would make fun of you if they discovered that you meditate?
- Where do you think Misa learned to meditate?

NUTRITION

It is disturbing to hear reports suggesting that our children are becoming increasingly overweight and are spending less time participating in physical activities. Schools have a responsibility to make nutrition and physical activities a priority in their curriculum.

Nutrition is about balance and moderation. There is truth to the adage "we are what we eat." Eating poorly affects our moods and can make some people prone to anger outbursts. Similarly, eating poorly makes us tired, irritable, restless, and more likely to make poor decisions.

Additional questions for discussion:
- Why is healthy eating good for us?
- Is eating too little just as bad as eating too much?
- Have you ever noticed that when you eat poorly you get tired and irritable?
- Why do athletes not eat junk food before they exercise or before a game?
- What does the phrase "you are what you eat" mean to you?

ORGANIZED

There is a strong relationship between being organized and performing better in school and extra-curricular activities. Kids who are organized tend to be more responsible and have more time to do things they enjoy. Alternatively, children who are poorly organized get easily distracted and often don't complete homework.

Children can practice organizational skills by keeping their desk and locker tidy. An organizer or assignment notebook is another useful way to keep track of things that need to be done. Organization takes practice and commitment.

Additional questions for discussion:
- What are the benefits of being organized?
- What are the problems associated with being disorganized?
- Why do kids who are disorganized tend to lose things more often?
- How can you help a friend become more organized?
- How can being more organized make you a better student?

PROBLEM SOLVING

Problem solving is an important technique to teach children and is particularly helpful in reducing anger. Research tells us that good problem solvers are more confident, have positive social behaviors, do well in school, and have healthier peer relationships. Problem solving involves the following steps:

- Identify the problem.
- Collect and summarize relevant information.
- Generate possible solutions.
- Anticipate the consequences for these solutions.
- Choose a solution based on best evidence.
- Review and assess.

Additional questions for discussion:

- How can you identify the real problem that needs to be solved??
- Who could help you generate solutions?
- Why is it important to anticipate consequences?
- Why do kids get angry whey they can not solve a problem?
- How would you help a friend who is having difficulties solving a problem?

QUIT

Sometimes children have a difficult time accepting losing. They like to win because this makes them feel good about themselves and because we praise them for winning. However, when they are losing they feel inadequate because they believe that they were not good enough. Some kids simply do not have the mechanism for dealing with disappointments. They get angry, become disruptive, and often quit before the activity is over. It's almost as if they prefer to be known as a quitter than a loser.

It is important that we teach children through role modeling how to be a gracious loser (as well as a gracious winner).We also need to help children understand that it is okay to lose. The important life skill that they need to master is perseverance. Finally we need to emphasize the effort over the outcome. We need children to understand that playing fairly within the rules and making an effort is as important as winning.

Additional questions for discussion:

- What does "being a sore loser" mean?
- Why do you think some kids get angry when they lose a game?
- What does it mean to be a bad winner?
- What does it mean to be a gracious loser?
- What should you do when you are angry because you are losing in a game?
- What should you do when other people get angry because they are losing in a game?

RUMORS

Spreading rumors is a typical response to being angry, upset or jealous of another person. Some children and adults who spread falsehoods enjoy doing it for fun. Unfortunately many children are not aware of the potential emotional hurt they cause when they start or perpetuate a rumor. Remind them that rumors are based on untruths and that spreading them can damage their reputation. Encourage students to ignore rumors even though this is difficult.

It is important to talk periodically about rumors and their potential consequences. Highlight the fact that rumors are not based on fact but rather on a distortion of the facts to hurt or embarrass someone.

Additional questions for discussion:

- Why do you think kids start rumors?
- Do you think it is okay to start a rumor about someone you do not like?
- Do you think spreading rumors is a form of bullying?
- What is the best way to respond to rumors?
- If you hear a rumor about a friend, what should you do?

SASSY

Some words that have the same meaning as sassy are "smart aleck," "cheeky," "lippy," "back talker," and "mouthy." Sassy behavior is annoying, belittling, sarcastic, and can be hurtful to others. It is a common response from children who are angry or upset with an adult. It can also be the result of seeking attention. Regardless of its origin, sassy behavior is never welcome. This is a behavior that needs to be challenged and stopped.

Additional questions for discussion:

- How do you think adults feel when children are sassy?
- Why do you think kids like Samuel feel they need to be sassy to get attention?
- What is the connection between sassiness and angry behavior?
- How can being sassy hurt someone's feelings?

TIME-OUT

A time-out is an effective strategy to help a child calm down. In sports, time-outs are used to stop play so a team can regroup and plan what they want to do next. In life, we can all use time-outs as a way to regain control of our thoughts and feelings and consider our choices. Time-outs are not meant to be punitive. The key is to develop a time-out plan with the child. This plan should answer questions, such as:

- When should the child take a time-out?
- Where should the child go?
- What is the duration of a time-out?
- What should the child do when returning to class?

Additional questions for discussion:

- Why do teams take a time-out during a game?
- What should you think about when you are in a time-out?
- What should you do when you are in a time-out?
- What should you do when you return from a time-out?
- How would you like your classmates to treat you after a time-out?

UNCOOPERATIVE

All children are uncooperative from time to time, and in many cases a simple reminder is all that is required. Being uncooperative might be due to tiredness, a need to be silly, or a desire to show off. Sometimes kids are uncooperative because they are afraid that others may discover that they cannot be successful in an activity. For kids, it is better to be seen as uncooperative rather than as incompetent. Teachers must survey the situation and determine the underlying reason for the uncooperative behavior.

Additional questions for discussion:

- Why do you think kids are sometimes uncooperative?
- How do you feel when someone is uncooperative and is preventing you from having fun?
- Do you think that some kids are uncooperative because then cannot do an activity?
- How can you help a friend become more cooperative?

VWX

Often the best solutions are those we discover for ourselves, such as selecting a favorite activity to calm down when angry. Being angry can be emotionally and physically exhausting and we need an opportunity to rejuvenate and charge our batteries.

Additional questions for discussion:

- Describe your feelings, thoughts after an anger episode.
- How can your friends be helpful to you after an anger episode?
- What are some ways you can calm down before you really get angry?
- What do you like to do after you get angry?

YELLING

Yelling is a typical response when a child is angry. However, there are times when children raise their voices because of excitement or fun. We need to make a distinction and act accordingly.

In this story, yelling is clearly a sign of frustration and anger. Yelling is often connected to feelings of helplessness and the inability to find a solution to a problem. We need to send a message to children that yelling is ineffective and counterproductive. We also need to model alternative behaviors such as listening, being attentive, and talking in a manner that conveys respect and trust.

Additional questions for discussion:

- Why do you think some kids yell more than others do?
- Do you think adults yell for the same reasons as kids?
- What does speaking with an "inside voice" mean?
- Why does yelling scare people?
- Do you think yelling is a good way to get your point across?

ZANY

Being zany bubbles up from the child in all of us. We need to find ways to nurture and celebrate acts of zanyness among adults and children. Simply put, zany behavior makes life enjoyable. These are the things that make us laugh and the things we do to make others laugh. We must encourage spontaneity and creativity in children so they can have fun in school. Enjoy joke telling and story telling and, from time to time, do the unusual. The key is to differentiate zany behavior that is humorous from behavior that is hurtful, embarrassing, or simply inappropriate.

Additional questions for discussion:

- What is the difference between doing something zany and doing something that is inappropriate?
- What does it feel like to be zany?

- What is the difference between doing something that is zany and doing something on a dare?
- When is being zany inappropriate?

About the Authors and Illustrator

Ray Ali (M.A.)

Ray is the lead writer and is a seasoned marriage and family therapist. He consults with schools and social service organizations and facilitates workshops on a wide range of topics including anger. His first book is titled *Chillout! Taming Anger: A Guide for Parents and Their Teens.*

Linda Sander (M.Ed.)

Linda is a school guidance counselor and is currently completing her master's degree in school psychology.

Jason Kroetsch (B.Ed.)

Jason has been an early childhood classroom teacher for the past eight years.

Eric Olson

Eric is a freelance illustrator based in Winnipeg, Canada. Since 1990 his work has appeared in an assortment of international publications.